The Great American Pyramid Scheme

Poems by

The Nü Profit$ of P/o/e/t/i/c Di$-chord

OAC Books
Belle, MO
osageac.org

OAC BOOKS
OSAGE ARTS COMMUNITY

Copyright © Jason Ryberg, W. E. Leathem,
Timothy Tarkelly, Mackenzie Thorn, 2022
First Edition: 1 3 5 7 9 10 8 6 4 2
ISBN: 978-1-952411-99-1
LCCN: 2022935466

Author photos: Will Leathem, Riley Werner-Leathem,
Timothy Tarkelly, Madison Thorn
All rights reserved. No part of this publication may be reproduced or transmitted in any form or by any means, electronic or mechanical, including photocopying, recording or by info retrieval system, without prior written permission from the author.

Acknowledgments:

Jason Ryberg: Special thanks to the editors of these publications where some of these poems previously appeared:

Borderless Journal, Fixator Press, Poetry Pacific, Piker Press, Danse Macabre, Lothlorien Poetry Journal, Locust Review, Ink Pantry Journal, Trailer Park Quarterly, River Dog Zine #3

W.E. Leathem: Some places brew a certain magic. For me, it is the used bookshop at 39th & Bell. Its mark has been indelible. Prospero's has inspired, colored and allowed for one of the finest lives one could imagine. These poems have been pulled from across that quarter century arc, with three having made their fledgling appearance in the very first Spartan chapbook: *Prospero's Pocket Poets Vol. 1.* To list all would fill its own book, but here's to Prospero's and all the souls who not only called it home, but whose shared adventures made it what it is. To the prime movers: Tom Wayne, Jason Ryberg, Kale Baldock, Brandon Whitehead, Rex Noland and John Condra. And especially those who've flown sorties behind the counter: Sophie Vic, Tera Duncan, Hammond Robinson, Jessica Rousseau, Blue Owl Hooser, Riley Werner-Leathem, Leslie Johns, Jordon Johns, Jim Sullivan, Dennis Helsel, and most recently Shawn Howard, Katie Szalay and Danny Mac Stayton. Thanks to the late Larry Ferlinghetti for allowing us to homage his Pocket Poets.

Timothy Tarkelly: Special thanks to Iain, who has already heard these stories.

Mack Thorn would like to thank Alien Buddha Press and is mostly just happy to be able to get a decent cortado, now and then.

TABLE OF CONTENTS

Jason Ryberg

Many Things Wonderful to Tell / 1

Some Distant Point / 2

Teardrop Repairs / 3

This American Thing / 4

Just a Little Fog or Rain in the Wind / 5

The Pig Less Travelled / 6

Nine Black Butterflies on a Propane Tank / 7

Portrait of Sky, Wind, Trees and Dog / 8

My Special Place / 9

Death Motif / 11

Time is / 15

Hangin' Out at the Git and Go / 16

All Throughout the Day / 17

A Place to Crash / 18

Ritual / 19

Still-Life of Blue Jay Sitting on a Broken-Down
  Refrigerator / 20

The Buddha Comes to Belle, MO / 21

Meaner Than the Devil on a Slow Day / 23

Diamonds and Embers / 25

W.E. Leathem

Winded / 29

Regimen & Heredity / 30

Morning Spent / 33

Dead Set Against / 34

Let's / 39

You Just Keep / 41

Whar's Teddy? / 43

Small Rooms / 45

Motion Sickness / 48

Hotelier Particulier / 50

A Dream of Donkeys / 52

Timothy Tarkelly

Iowa Workshop Model / 57

Concerning Apocalypse / 59

Jackie's Type / 60

Frisco Burger / 61

OETR / 62

Olathe / 63

Apology or Something Like It / 64

Texas Martini / 65

Columbus / 66

The Wedding Is Over / 67

Anger Management / 68

In Hays, American On a Thursday / 69

Okay, Okay You Were Right / 70

Sunrise / 72

Porching It Up / 73

Between Izumo and Your Bedroom / 74

Will You Sign My Yearbook / 75

Genesis / 76

Stuck In the Middle / 77

Cacti / 78

Rivertowne / 79

Gardening Tools / 80

Summer / 81

Mack Thorn

One Armed Forklift Driver / 85

Whatever You Do Don't Get Old / 86

A Noble Last Stand / 87

What Makes a Good Bar? / 89

Lift Kit Rain Dance / 90

Ruby Ridge / 91

Sky Levee / 93

Peoples Changes / 94

Roommates / 95

When My Well Went Dry / 96

Shake and Bake / 97

Animal / 99

I Hate My Screen Door / 100

Hunger and Loneliness / 101

Bus Stop Advice / 102

A Sunny Kansas Afternoon / 103

Red Meat Causes Alzheimer's / 104

Pistol Whip Neurons / 106

You Got it All Wrong Kid / 107

The Great American Pyramid Scheme / 108

Lost Track of Time / 109

Nobody's from here
Most of us just live here
Locals long since moved away
Sold their played-out farms for parking lots
Went off looking for a better way
Onto some bright future somewhere
Better times on down the road
Wonder if they ever got there
Wherever it was they thought they'd go

-James McMurtry

Jason Ryberg

Jason Ryberg was born in the heart of a parade only to be abandoned, days later, on the steps of what turned out to be (what some people might describe as somewhat serendipitously) the meeting place for a secret and arcane society of wealthy gentlemen werewolves, by whom he was raised, though, to his knowledge, never initiated, fully, into all of their arcane ways, but still considered to be a full and honored member of the tribe, in good standing, and so he was then sent to the finest schools, where, over time, he became quite a renown poet and respected philosopher before the age of 22, and with many promising career and social prospects, but instead, gave it all up for a life of adventure - fortunes and glory the likes of which historians and poets, professors and philosophers would discuss and debate for centuries to come.

Many Things Wonderful to Tell

The mad monkish scientist of jazz
sits smiling at the grand unveiling of his

latest creation, while a railroad bridge
riveted together of mostly weathered

driftwood and old rusty pieces of scrap
iron shows us the nearest way to many

possible futures where, amongst many
other things wonderful to tell in this

hot and swampy Sargasso sea of broken-
down cars, campers, bicycles and boats,

a lone pristine Cadillac sits, ready for
lift-off, to take us to what all the locals

swear is the best damn greasy spoon
diner in the galaxy.

Some Distant Point

There's a man with a blur for a face,
a can of beer and a cigarillo, standing

in a corner of a fancy living room, somewhere,
with a hardwood floor, a Persian rug and

an empty chair in the other, a bay window
between them, showing us a Spring day of

impressionist blues, yellows and greens
with a barbwire fence and an old dirt road,

trailing off to some distant point on the horizon,
and each post crowned with an old boot.

Teardrop Repairs

for John Dorsey and Victor Clevenger

The sign outside the shop read
TEARDROP REPAIRS, which
must have got all our minds firing.
collectively in, more or less, the same
direction because, all at once, we tell
the cab driver to turn around to which
he replied *it's your dime, pal, 85 cents
a mile,* and the next thing you know,
we're just sitting there, parked in front
of the place for who knows how long,
in this sweaty-ass cab with shitty AC
and meter running, in the middle of
a summer day, just off the two lane
highway that runs right through the
middle of St. John, KS, until we finally
start to comprehend and the spell is
suddenly lifted and we laugh because,
of course, it's not a repair shop for
broken teardrops.

This American Thing

So, just what do we make of this whole
peculiar and particular thing of ours
that so many have tried to identify,
dissect and analyze over the years,

this nebulous and amorphous thing we've
only ever managed to assign a slippery,
side-stepping, deflective designation to,
instead of its own proper name (as the
Chinese say, *to each and everything...**)

this not wholly abstract thing that otherwise
remains at-large out there in a most likely
unstable state wherein it may, at any given
moment, degenerate further into little more
than a cheap substitute for Harvey the rabbit
or stunt double for Schrodinger's neon elephant
(always stinking up our national living room
with its toxic, effluvial Trumpeting),

neither of which has anybody here-to-fore
been able to consistently confirm or deny
whether they are, indeed, despite the obvious
destruction left in their wake, even a thing at all.

**Ancient Confucian Maxim: The beginning of wisdom
is first to give each and everything its proper name.*

Just a Little Fog or Rain in the Wind

It was just an old-fashioned style streetlamp
that the city must have decided was worth
investing in (it and another hundred more
or so just like it)

for some kind of downtown, main street
renovation plan, way back when, who knows
how many years ago.

But it had kind of an exotic, old-timey charm to it,
and the way they all lit up the downtown area,
the side-streets, especially, late at night,
or with a little fog or rain in the wind,
gave our quaint, prairie town more of what some of us
imagined to be a hip Portland / 'Frisco feel to it,
maybe just a bit of New Orleans or Paris, even.

places most of us had only read about
in magazines and books or seen in movies,
but possibly, a few had actually visited, once,

maybe even came close to getting wrapped up in,
losing themselves and never returning home.

The Pig Less Travelled

And if you find that you've come to a place
seeking enlightenment, change or merely asylum,

maybe even the minimal requisite velocity
necessary to break the gravitational bonds of

your own life, and you find yourself one morning,
6 or 7am, drinking coffee and staring off at some

arbitrary point on the horizon, and suddenly a man
in a truck drives up, a man who has the mildly deranged

look of a man all too familiar with the revolving door of
the incarceration process and he asks you if you'd like to

help him ketch a pig up on Highway D, and even though
you're only wearing boxers and a t-shirt and you haven't

even had more than a couple of sips of coffee and no time
to think at all, you say... *yes, of course I would.*

Nine Black Butterflies
on a Propane Tank

There's nine black butterflies
> resting on the spine of a silver
>> propane tank, beneath the shady

over-hang of a linden tree,
> everything dripping and glistening
>> in the sun, which has just now

come back out again
> after a brief morning thundershower,
>> allowing us to resume the solemn ritual

of black coffee and brown sugar and
> the making of lists of things to do today
>> that may or may not ever get done.

Portrait of Sky, Wind, Trees and Dog

The sky is the color
of an old primer-gray Camaro,
with a few rusted-out spots, here and there,
where someone has done a messy job of patching them up.

And the wind is a sorrowful, moaning chorus of ghosts,
who are attempting to do a post-modernist rendition
of an old Russian opera.

And the trees are all doing their
leaning-this-way-and-that, stretching-out-the-stiffness-
and-kinks, catching-up-on-all-the-latest-gossip-thing.

And a dog, with a stake and chain still attached
and trailing from his collar, making a rather comical,
klinkity-klanking soundtrack for his big escape scene,
trots, joyously, down the slick, leaf-plastered street,
his former life of incarceration already mostly forgotten.

My Special Place

It's a cold, dank sad-
song-about-somethin'-that-went-
wrong-kind o' place, where

phone calls from nowhere
still come in for people who don't
live there anymore

but no one ever
comes to visit, and the sump-
pumps are always backed-

up with clumps of check-
stubs and lottery tickets,
the dregs of bad dreams

and expectations
that were diminished before
they were even born.

And all the lights here
are mostly burned out (or just
flickering) except

for one old greasy
mechanic's lamp hangin' there
by a long yellow

cord (that's just outside
the door) and one 60-watt
bulb swingin' gently

on the end of a
string above the sink. And it
is a dirty and

indifferent light
that they cast and no one
can say what happened.

Death Motif

I've often dreamed
of Death as a bullet from
a gun in the hand

of some dumb *fucko*
sticking up a Quick Trip at
1am who has

decided that he,
suddenly, just doesn't like
something about me;

Death as a pale and
rider-less horse, without a
warning and for no

reason apparent
to me, kicking my brains deep
into next week, or

as a carving knife
plunged into my pumpkin-like
head by a woman

who has finally
reached her point of critical
mass with me, or a

twenty car pile-up
on an iced-over highway
late at night or an

airplane suddenly
stripping a gear or throwing
a rod and then free-

falling into the
ocean. I have envisioned
Death as haplessly

bobbing along some-
where at sea and waiting for
one or more of its

inhabitants to
take an interest in me;
Death as the edge of

a thirty-story
building, somehow teasing me
closer and closer

to it (for just a
little peak, no doubt in deep
collusion with my

curiosity
and (post-post-) adolescent
fascination with);

Death as the gaping,
jagged maw of a Grizzly
Bear, suddenly just

appearing in my
path on a leisurely stroll
through a landscape where,

here-to-fore, no bears
of any kind have ever
actually been

seen, Death as a slow-
motion and mutually
assured nuclear

holocaust, repeating,
over and over again,
on an endlessly

looping strip, Death as
crazed stalker or nemesis
from my past, at long

last catching up to
me as I stumble home from
the bar, Death as an

otherwise highly
curable disease or some
severe injury

and me just one more
of the 1/3 of (meaning
100,000,000)

Americans with-
out any health insurance
or savings, Death as

a serious mis-
understanding between me
and a SWAT team that's

kicking my door in
at 4 in the morning. But,
as a matter of

fact, I have never,
ever pictured or dreamed of
Death as hooded grim

reaper character
or devilishly dapper
dude at the wheel of

a hearse, patiently
waiting for me to get my
affairs in order.

Time is

time was,
>	time will
most likely
>	forever be (if
the experts
>	are to be
believed),
>	at least until
that fateful
>	time when
there's no one
>	left to be
of a mind
>	to ask or
tell anyone
>	else
what time it
>	is.
Not a single
>	soul.
So, there
>	you go,
sleep tight,
>	sweet dreams…

Hangin' Out at the Git and Go

The moon tonight
is the lone pink sodium street light
of one more no name, gas station /
grain elevator town with no bar,
no diner, no movie theater
(since 1980-something),

nothing to do on a Friday
or a Saturday night but get
into trouble in some other town
the next county over, or hang out
here, at the Git and Go,

and watch a few cars passing through;
sometimes some outta town types
pull in to gas up and walk around a while,
stretching and joking,

asking themselves, each other
and, finally, one of us

where the hell are we?

All Throughout the Day

Steam is rising up
from the newly
laid tarmac on HWY D
after a brief but intense
summer thunder-shower
this morning that came
and went before the sun
could even slip behind
a cloud, and the radio is
telling us to *expect similar
activity all throughout
the day, and now it's back
to the music with Tommy
James and the Shondells
doing "Crimson and Clover,"*
and I say hell yes to the
prospects of both more
Tommy James and the
Shondells in all our lives
as well as more sporadic
bursts of thunder and
lightning and rain while
the sun continues to
shine, brightly,
throughout
the day.

A Place to Crash

I went to the porch
thinking I would see rain but
instead it was the

wind blowing the last
of the leaves of the season
out of the trees (still

stubbornly clinging
to their branches) and out in-
to the wider world

to find a place to
crash and lay low 'til things calmed
down a little, now

that Old Man Winter
(that mean, old bastard) was back
from his over the

road gig and just might
be thinking about hanging
around for a while.

Ritual

Five fat, sleepy flies,
treading around in the last
millimeter of

sugary pink stuff
at the bottom of a tall
bottle of what the

label says is *fine
sparkling rosé mascatto*—
comfortable with

their fate or simply
incapable, it would seem,
of conceiving of

mortality in
either the abstract or the
concrete in even

the most primitive
sort of way, so, I shake them,
all, one by one by

one, out onto the
grass and let the ritual
begin once again.

Still-Life of Blue Jay Sitting on Broken-Down Refrigerator

I was sitting on the back porch
sipping on some sweat tea and bourbon
after a long day of hauling junk to the dump
and there's this big, sassy Blue Jay brazenly
perched and puffed-up on a busted refrigerator
we somehow missed earlier, and he's giving me
the stink eye, maybe even thinking

*what's up
with this guy, this no-flying, blah-blah-blah-
spewing, stomp-stomp-stomping around,
hairless, featherless, colorless clown with his
great big brain and fancy opposable thumbs,
but still always shitting in his own nest and
generally fucking things up for the rest of us
like he owned the place or something and we
we're all just a bunch of squatters...*

No, no old Poe
crow, this one, sitting on gleaming bust of Pallas
to torment my sleepless after-hours, but maybe
still some kind of generic, low-grade harbinger
of encroaching doom or ruffled beast of the
apocalypse.

And then he cackled a few more notes,
took a dump and fluttered up, up and away
and out of my life forever.

The Buddha Comes to Belle, MO

I have only just
recently noticed the old
             man sitting every

morning at the end
of his half-mile gravel drive,
             just outside of town,

in a sort of sling
seat he's somehow managed to
             Jerry-rig on to his

walker, in which he
will sit for hours, waving and
             smiling, in a sort

of blissed-out yet still
serene Buddha kind of way,
             at all the cars as

they roll in and out
of town, until the mailman
             finally arrives

with his truck full of
goodies, where it's always hit
             or miss these days, and

then they'll trade a few
jokes and some local gossip
                and then he'll shuffle

back to the house for
lunch and a quick nap, we can
                safely imagine.

Meaner Than the Devil on a Slow Day

Hell, I read the good
book, the Holy Bible, *the
word of the Lord,* and

if there is a god
like that and even half of
that shit is halfway

true, then he's a mean
motherfucker, way meaner
than the Devil, on

a slow day, even:
one of those big types always
answering *why* with

*because I said so,
that's why,* and it's their way and
no other, and they

want you doing what
they say, when they say it, not
what they do, not to

mention all the blood,
floods, locusts and plagues, the rapes
and the killing of

the first born male child
and *if you don't like it here,
you can go to hell.*

Diamonds and Embers

We all just sat there
out in my neighbor's backyard,
beneath the stars and

satellites, spy planes
and UFOs, laughing and
laughing as we watched

the bottle chase the
pipe chase the bottle 'round and
'round the bonfire in

hi-def, rollicking,
cartoonish HI-larity,
until the whole thing

inevitably
lost its manic momentum
and slowed to a halt,

leaving us nothing
but diamonds in our dreams and
embers at our feet.

W. E. Leathem

Founder and co-owner of Kansas City's famous independent bookstore, Prospero's, **w.e. leathem** has published three collections of poetry, numerous essays and short fictions. He lives in Missouri.

Winded

With a head like a pauper,
unfurl the crimson banner
to flail its foretelling
of an ending

Vices abandoning ship,
ears ringing in morning breeze,
the curse of regular employment
gawking one square in the eyes

Go on,
take your change
in fitful dreams,
exchanging hoped-for bliss
for the surer currency
of this instant's understanding

and though the kingdom
of heaven awaits, linger here
awhile longer among the pleasures
of *this* world

Regimen & Heredity
(that winning smile will take you places)

No cavities, here
No need for steel
nor rubber
Just a lifetime of:
before bed,
after breakfast,
and after each
and every meal

Regimen and heredity
bequeathing opportunity
or so foretells a slip
of paper birthed
of a cookie… (the *only*
source, really, once can
take to the bank)

There are places
I simply don't wanna go:

…for a ride
in back of a van
to talk with the men
(hooded or turbaned,
crossed or sickled,
woke or awake),

all equally determined
to take you swimming
in cement sneakers

…to warm a seat
in some classroom
or church on this bright
glory-filled morn

…to work
for my living

And I suppose
this can differ
from soul to soul,
but will these pearly whites
take me out to a ballgame
or to dinner and a night of dancing?

Will they steer me clear
of a lifetime of crime,
or bad investments
or the scale that lurks
by the shitter door
at 3 am?

Will they mitigate my appointment
with Ma'at's fabled feather?

More than likely,
this winning smile
will simply earn me
a little overtime
and a bill for late fees

What
  did
    you
      expect?

This row of bicuspids
couldn't even keep me
arm's distant from
diabolical fingers,
robed in rubber,
gleefully fumbling over
a shiny array of apparatus
belonging to
the Marquis' apprentice
      — the dentist

Morning Spent

Spent the morning reading
Damon Runyon and listening
to Porter Wagoner, tinny from
the speaker of my i-phone

Out of the blue, a memory:

Mom swaying in some
unseen breeze, unaware
that I watch from the other room.
Off key, she's humming
in that way she had, along to
Green Green Grass of Home,
as it plays on the transistor
radio in her pocket

Even now, she doesn't
seem to note just how
threadbare her dress is

Dead Set Against

for Dorothy

Vladimir Ilyich Lenin is dead

Chairman Mao — dead
Pol Pot — dead
Li Po — dead
(as is Teddy Roosefveldtt)

Daunte Wright
a simple mistake,
coulda happened to anyone…
dead at the scene

Perhaps not overly dramatic,
but Bertolt Brecht is certainly dead
Pavarotti — dead
Albert Einstein…difficult to fathom,
yet still dead

Russell E. Leathem
born July 4, 1913
Bosworth Missouri,
father of four, husband to two — now dead

Brünnhilde,
Simone de Beauvoir,
Golda Meir,

Edna St. Vincent Millay...
their spirits harried
by the masculine want
of the years
        all dead

Amelia Earhart — we have to suppose so

Jean Cocteau — dead
Inigo Jones — dead
Jan Vermeer — a picture's perfection of death

Ladies and Gentlemen,
   the President of these United States!
who, while perhaps not
technically *brain dead*
(and avoiding all the distasteful
discussion of just deserts),
will, one day, also be dead

Gandhi — dead
Mother Teresa — dead
Billy Sunday (go on, now
stop all that off-color funnin'
and endless discussin'
of where he'll be taking
of his eternal reward)

Seneca — dead
Copernicus — dead

Eli Whitney
    and Janis Joplin – dead

Many a winter, now,
beneath the sod
out back, laid to rest
against the fence
that hemmed him in,
ever-faithful Skippy,
my childhood friend

Christa McAuliffe — kaput!
Princes Di — a smashing exit!
(did you catch the pics?!)

Jeffrey Dahmer
got what was coming to 'im
(though don'tcha think,
don't we all?)

John Adams — clinging
to the failing light
had to be sure
his old enemy,
his old friend,
was first to board
that last train to Clarksville

The man in black
has been seen out back

chatting with that fellow in the hood,
and the word on the street
is Joey and Johnny and Dee Dee
wont be making the reunion tour

And lest we
get ahead of ourselves,
dear brother Carroll, who,
while he may know a few,
still has a few more drags
on his last cigarette
   Yet, one day…

Virginia went swimming
with her pockets full of rocks;
Sylvia poked her head in the stove —
though there are those who say
she may have had a little push,
psychologically speaking,
somewhere along the way…

Ernie and Kurt
and the good Dr. Thompson
all booked their own flights

Rock Hudson — dead
Kate Hepburn — dead
Liberace, always the dandy,
so fine in sequined red,
yet, like the proverbial door nail
remains extravagantly dead

and *your* voice, Mark
from down along youth's back yard,
still echoes across these years

Somewhere, a meter's running
In a pocket, a ticket as yet unpunched
but between you and me
(and the fencepost)
I'm not looking forward
to Ma'at and his fucking feather,
or Dante's and his proverbial
purgatorial scrub

And it may, just may
turn out, as the sand
dwindles in the glass,
that old age, is a prison sentence
for the terminally guilty
whose time for sinning is,
now, long past

Let's

Let us live like life is sure,
our footing without question
With our backs to the pit,
let us build our castle on the sands,
stalk desire across these borderlands

Let us take each breath suddenly,
inhale its violent accord,
set free the periodic perfection
that crawls up the leg of reflection
and remembering, dance
in pandemonium's halls

Let us live like breathing is terminal,
holding fast the perimeter's waning,
turn into the avalanche of approaching void

Let us live each day upside down,
sever the solar umbilical
Orphans from dusk til dawn,
let's start in the middle,
dive right in,
squirming and spinning,
desperately living
and so the ending begin

For I see the cold man standing
in the hall, his toe is tapping,
biding his time on the crest
of *no more to come*
Forgive me, we must make haste!
The tread of footsteps is near behind,
and the streets they fill with a rushing,
silent cacophony come to cut short
beauty's interlude

You Just Keep

Hey man,
don't push me
I'm already moseying
as fast as I care to,
as fast as I can

Excuse me as i wipe
the residue of
an unpardonable sin
from my lips,
and don't mind me
pecking at this carcass
lying across the center lane

I've done my part
to piss in the party punch,
to sniff at the rear end
of the moment slipping away

You, go on ahead,
swipe life's little plastic card
through the reader
at the cosmic check-out,
I think I forgot something
back in aisle 9 …

Yet, there you are (again),
breathing that stinky breath down my neck,
stepping all over my feet,
scuffing my shiny new kicks!
encroaching on my space,
making my decisions uncomfortable,
my comforts unlawful

And for what?
what about you
makes you think
you can tell someone like me
(or any of a million others)
what lines can and can't be crossed?

'Best back off
cause you're inconveniently
between me and a
road I've not yet taken

Besides,
what have you to show
that the hours bequeathed
by fate have not been
utterly wasted?

Whar's Teddy
(When You Need 'im...)

Shout hurrah to Erin go Braugh and all the yankee nations
~Theodore Roosevelt

Acting on
the good advice
of my trained medical practitioner,

in close counsel
with my portfolio manager,

under careful direction
of my certified tai chi trainer
and yoga coach,

pursuing wisdom
over a beer
in a bar
with a friend
on another lost
Saturday afternoon

Perilously close
to a train wreck,

strung out
along the aggregate
back roads
of this great land,

our identity's stolen,
all the capital gone

from our ideas,
from our pension plans,

the equity squandered in
a friendly game of spades
under the ever-watchful eyes
of the folk over in
> Sacramento,
> DC,
> Albany
> Jefferson City…

And the barons
are back in town again,
drooling over access,
in need of a swift boot
in the seat of their pants

Whar's Teddy,
whar's Teddy
whar's Teddy
> *when you need 'im…*

Small Rooms

Down from the apartments,
from the bed-sits and duplexes,
down stairwells
and the dimly lit corridors,

hurrying at the day's final fading

Up urgent streets,
bats at sunset,
oyamel-hungry monarchs
indentured to millennia-old instincts

Inuit, trudging in sealskin boots,
crossing the narrow dilemma
between another evening in
and that bench-warrant ardor
to pull close dusky collars
against the first seasonal flurries of
oh, how i hate to be alone

Brightly-lit,
holiday furloughs,
now rescinded:

a photo fading on the fridge,
its last, receding echo
of temperate, after-hours breezes

purchased on lay-away,
stowed in the freezer
like a snowball,
for later

Hours, pleading absolution
from neon priests,
incant in earnest
against the severe length
of evenings

Lingering in bookstore aisles
Gathered on coffee shop sofas
stirring steaming cups of doubt
Struggling with the crossword
or huddled over chess boards

refugees from
the dampness that gathers
in the cob-webbed
corners of solitude,
clamor's expatriates
just within earshot
of smoky conversations

orphans of the solstice
distracted by the angular
daylight-savings ache

abandoned, alone
awaiting inspiration's inebriated saunter
in the bell-wrung stupor
that decants from every door

Not the best of company, perhaps
But company none the less

Motion Sickness

What once was up,
now is down, was *in*
is now out of favor.
And the tragically hip,
those sweet young things
who dared to be cool,
have taken day jobs
to labor for their pleasures

But don't sweat it none.
The cocktail galleries
opening-night teem
with black-sweltered honey's
carrying keys to daddy's condo
And their coffee shop conversation,
if accompanied with libation
and the promise of wet panties,
will help ease the pain
of the suspected truth

So, go on and smile,
have another gulp of wine,
knowing all the while
that over your shoulder
lurks the notion, a terrible
ocean of creeping doubt,
that maybe it's high time
that bags were packed

and the lanes again, dusty
beneath one's feet

Standing here before,
feet on this very space
of floor, knowing
what must be done,
though the thought of it
makes one just a little queasy

New spaces and new faces,
calling one foot out before the next
Faster and faster the pace,
to keep distant, to hold safe
the sure, numbing ache
of time an place n love's passing…

It's a shame, you know
At first, this one did seem different.
But somehow, somewhere
  something changed
And the edge no longer comes
to the blade, no matter
how hard you grind
And there's that sinking feeling,
leaning in close behind
to whisper in your ear:

Your time here
    has just about
        run out

Hotelier Particulier

> *... to shake the wainscot where the field-mouse trots*
> ~ T.S. Eliot

I.
A corpse at 12 Rue Oudinot,
in a basement a stone's throw
from the Prime Minister's manse,
30 years mouldering. The long
dead again putting the kibosh
an the plans of the living

II.
Nail houses, running
to seed, tattered
and threadbare,
shabby cousins confronting
towering glass and steel
Nowhere to run, lone
students facing down
Tiananmen's tank,
they stiffen their upper lips,
cinch up their griddles
against the looming
ravenous development

III.

Take nothing but pictures,
leave nothing but footprints
in the dust. Urban ramblers,
spelunking the shuttered and crumbling
edifices decreed *private,*
risk arrest, in order to
be the last to view,
the first to capture
a final snapshot from
the soon-to-be-razed

IV.

The softest hands, it's said,
belong to Master Zhou,
in the hard-pack dirt
near the Yellow River,
his trowel and soft brush
Passé these days
the Maoist relic-smashing
At 5,300 years,
the lineage of humanity's longest
unbroken civilization

A Dream of Donkeys

Again, the donkeys
braying in the valley,
and the opium moon,
a lock of dreams fallen
across its brow, weeps
like a heart sundered
beneath the willows

From the mantel
a vase has toppled,
the urn in which we keep our days
And remorseful fingers rummage
the cinder and the soot for one
recognizable shard of lips
once alive with hellos

And the tungsten friendships,
forged in pool halls
and at the bottom
of glasses, cinch up
their belts to have another go
at the Lazarus loves
that do not fade

All the while,
through the open door,
night pools on the floor,

laps against my feet,
toes wiggling in the shallows
where the herons feed

And as god leans in to kiss my lips,
the donkeys, below in the valley,
will not cease their braying

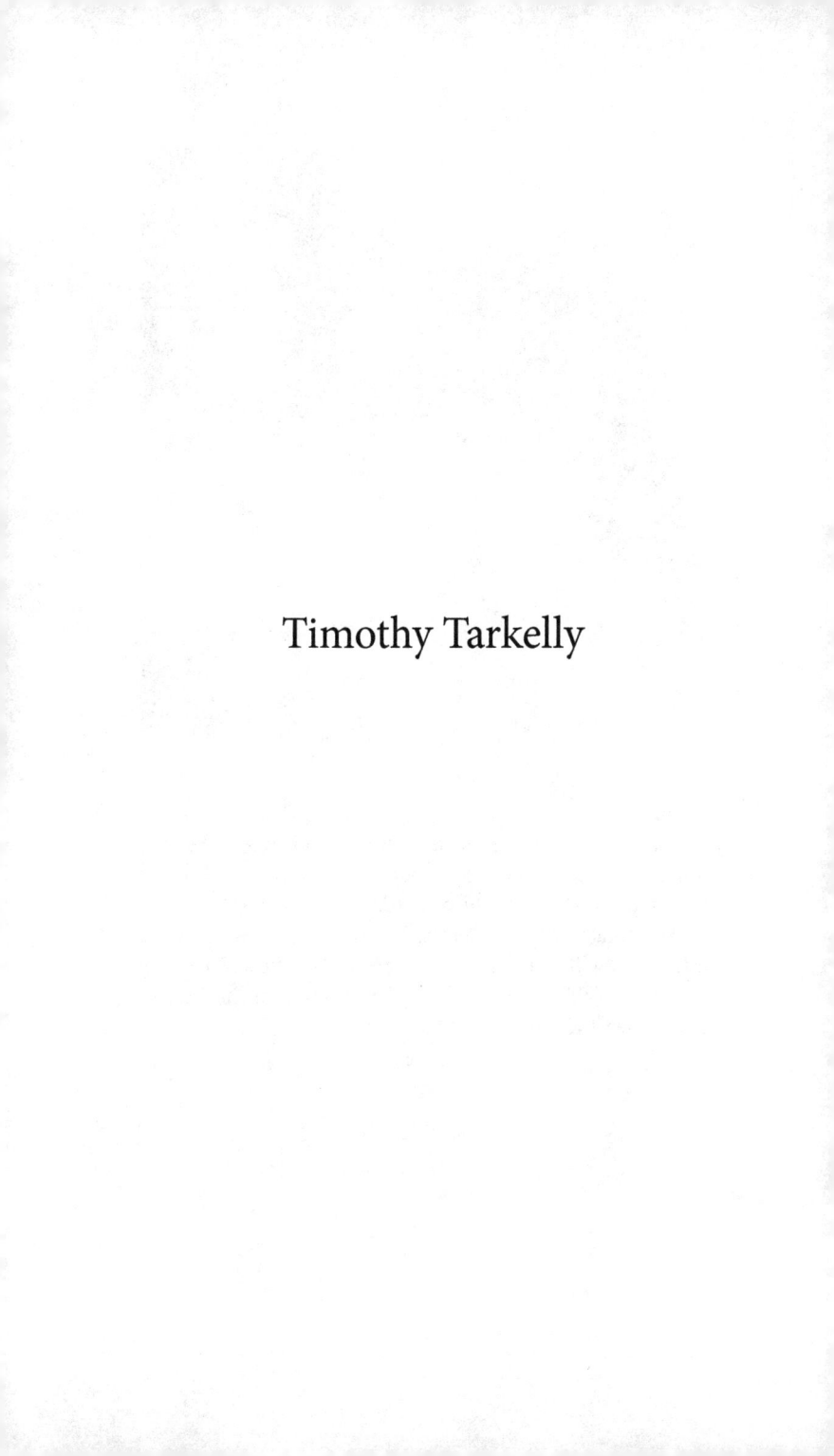

Timothy Tarkelly

Timothy Tarkelly's work has appeared in *Flyover Country, The Jupiter Review, The Daily Drunk,* and others. He has published several books of poetry including *Luckhound* (Spartan Press) and *On Slip Rigs and Spiritual Growth* (OAC Books). Most recently, he collaborated with visual artist Elena Samarsky on the book *All Other Forms of Expression* (OAC Books.) When he's not writing, he teaches in Southeast Kansas.

IOWA WORKSHOP MODEL

No, I don't want to talk
about eye opening adjectives, about craft.
I want to tell you what it's like
to drown
in front of everyone.
And how if you scream and fight
fifty feet below the surface
of your own shortcomings
it just looks like you're dancing.

The thing is,
we sculpt our stories into songs
and pretend we are elevating language
by calling our red blood crimson
and praising each sunrise
as god's newest beginning,
by thatching nets out of our hang-ups
and dragging them along the bottom
of our most recent memories.

We inject humor because we know
our families will laugh
and let our cries for help
hover just beyond their attention span.
We use imagery to hide
how window-streaked and grimy
our perspectives really are.

Maybe, we'd be better off
recanting our embarrassments
to a professional,
instead of this circle. Storyteller's
are liars by nature, absorbing each other's pain
just to wring out their bodies, let it all drip
into crudely formed stanzas with their name
neatly tucked under the title.

For once, let's just say what we mean.
Spend more time on healing,
less time sweating
over line breaks.

CONCERNING APOCALYPSE

Some say the world will end in a Robert Frost poem,
some say in moderation, bit by bit.
I'd wager we never get much further
than the regular, lukewarm destruction,
just lying around when we should be tightening the screws
that keep this carousel turning,
in bed with the wrong people,
the tall tales, tall liars,
a poisoned apple and sleepy sex appeal.
Remember that one guy?
You thought, swore it, it wasn't serious
and then you were crying,
calling from a stairwell?
That's where it'll all go down.
The world will burn
while you come to your senses
on the cold, dirty floor. And we'll curse
the tile of all things, we'll say we called it,
saw it coming from a mile away
and retreated into our blankets.
Just got comfy with our habits,
just let them take right over.

JACKIE'S TYPE

She turned me down and latched onto a son
of the Dakotas, two bodies that had come together
to shape him from the rocks, from the cow punch leather,
from Stetson felt. Blessed him with a wandering spirit
that took him all of ten feet, dropped him with a dull thud
right in the middle of everyone else's good time,
but granted him a chin christened with sharp charm,
an eternity of yesterday's stubble.

Lonely coyote moons followed him around
just to set behind him, making each dumb thing
he said sound like the credits were about to roll
and I'm not saying I couldn't have taken him,
but it would've meant doing him a favor.
No one wore grit, bruises, and wild like he did,
and boy, did she love to kiss on his wounds,
nurse him back to weight, back to barfighting health.

FRISCO BURGER

for Jason Ryberg

Not all leaps of faith are so rewarding,
they don't all come with cheese.
But expectation is getting easy to defeat
in this land of wandering children,
of cellphone signal so faint
it's crushed under the slightest hint of urgency.
And frankly, I prefer not to be asked
how I like my burgers cooked.
You either know there's only one right answer,
or you wouldn't be able to deliver
my version of pink in the middle anyway.
Historically, perspective has been shaped
by fuel far worse than silence, griddle grease,
a stomach spoiled by its own sensitivities.
We should all take leaps of faith more often.

OETR

For Rebecca

Can't tell if it's the mucinex
or my hangover talking,

but I'm glad you're laughing.
I'm trying to build a single thought

from absent pieces,
elusive crumbs fallen from old dictionaries

as you insist that small words
are much bigger than their parts.

My brain and its sister nerves
are sentenced, marched to the gallows.

No final words,
just heavy eyes

and a bloodshot thirst
for the obvious.

OLATHE

Crying in a hotel lobby,
clutching my chest
as the last few plucks of my will
strain and heave. I can feel
the borders of my humanity shift,
the clear coated restraint
that keeps me in step, keeps me from
taking this out on everyone around me,
chucking vases and strangers' bags
into the parking lot,
letting it all die in one brittle swoop.
Carrion feathers forever marking
the last time we tried to do things ourselves.

APOLOGY OR SOMETHING LIKE IT

Picking excuses from Grecian vines
splayed along half-baked remedies for a good time.
Plot holes, unnecessary height,
traditions steeped in grape-stained feet
and – almost always – drunken tantrums
that would put Noah's nakedness to shame.

That's when it hurts the most,
these moments the old us
would've reveled in,
admired life's odd cycles.
We would've sworn that we'd be next,

clad in silk and reborn

at the end of spring.

TEXAS MARTINI

I love most breakfast food, but
people actually put spinach in their eggs?
Hell, I knew a guy who'd ash his cigarette
right into his beer. I thought,
if you have to look that hard for a challenge,
then man, it must be great to be alive.
A life so soft you have to sharpen the edges,
man, it must be great to be alive, to be alive.

COLUMBUS

We had both lived in the same town at different
times, and wouldn't you know it, we still walk around
with the same favorites, the same restaurants, the
same blue plates hovering over our tongues like
holy question marks. Remember Ruth Anne's?
Fresh catfish? And how the word tea used to mean
something? How beer hits different in the Georgia
summer and man, it would have been great if we
could have shared a plate of frog legs, fried squirrel
ten years earlier, back when we were still whistling to
the future we built in our heads, still seeing the forest
for the meat crawling in the trees.

THE WEDDING IS OVER
For Tyler

We walked Orlando around the parking lot,
aired him out and got him in the car,
Wichita, as a whole, came together to tell us no,
wag its finger at our late night musings
on adventurous spirits and volume.
And when we got settled at the hotel,
it was my turn to stomp around,
trip over life itself and ramble on,
an incoherent tirade about how alcohol
has no power over me.

It's good that you're always the designated driver,
always willing to take the defeated home,
put us to bed and stand watch,
eat your leftover Chinese food
until you're certain we've succumbed
to a healing slumber,
saving every I-told-you-so
for the morning.

ANGER MANAGEMENT

The Braves are losing and while I usually rub it in, I can feel something coming. There's a pebble loose in the driveway, waiting to be caught in someone's sipes and sent through the living room window. Your hand keeps turtling, turning into a red fist, then loosening itself before anyone notices. Except that we all notice, and I'd ask, but sometimes anger deserves a little dignity of its own. For now, we will let the steam fester in the holding tank until it loses its appetite for bursting, gives up on itself, loses its vaporous stride and just drips. Drips like lazy, old tears. We'll talk about it then.

IN HAYS, AMERICA ON A THURSDAY
for Anja

I'm ordering another,
discussing denim at great length,
everything it has to say about form,
curves contained by ardorous thread
and cut-off audacity.
 I feel full – beer has always been
my worst idea – but regret
is just a catchall, a word we think
we are supposed to use,
though pain often comes
with angelic rewards,
like a few moments
with this night's brightest star
hanging under the ninth sign,
slumming it in Western Kansas,
talking about sage bundles
and organic independence.
 I wish we could light this place up,
cull good vibes from the fumes,
clear the air of every last
troublesome thought,
leave us with nothing
but the smell of singed herbs,
chilled glasses,
and a promise
that I won't say anything too weird.

OKAY, OKAY, YOU WERE RIGHT

You say it won't be worth it, but how could we walk away
from a scene so happy? Tab out for this? Cable TV?
I can't focus, the memory of everyone's laughter
is buzzing louder than the reruns, when did we start
trading bars for lobbies? Little lonely rooms
with ugly furniture and a water dispenser,
cookie-cutter cucumber slices floating, failing to bring
    a sense of adventure
to another boring attempt at easing my faculties.

I bet they're still there,
a whole bar full of smiling people,
of game day TVs that only show victory,
of a bartender who may or may not have been flirting
    with you, but man, could she pour a drink,
exactly the right way, the away-from-home-and-I-just-got-
    paid way.

Let's go back, we'll practice our entrance
in the elevator, make a show of our return.
Let's let the morning serve whatever justice it wants
for our purposeful slog of hunger and hubristic second
    winds.

You say it won't be worth it,
but spontaneity make its own convincing argument,
is dressed in an impressive suit,
swirling one of those drinks in her hand. She's calling you

chicken and I am, too. You say it won't be worth it,
but listen. Hand me the keys
to the next few hours of your life,
and I'll deliver you to the doorstep
of demonstrable, tangible happiness.

When have I ever steered us wrong?

SUNRISE

When I tell you I'm lonely,
I don't just mean this night's a little quiet,
that memories are ringing happier times
while Tuesday evening does its thing.
I mean that my chest is rattling
like a storm window missing all but one
of its screws, that I'm one bad breath away
from disaster.
My neighbors are either deep sleepers,
or unconcerned. If the only thing I can hear
is my own voice, then I'm going to hear it,
full tilt, fuck the cones, blow the speakers.
I spend a lot of time thinking
about broken glass, mirrors as they crumble,
picture frames that were never meant
to hang in one place that long.
My skin has always been soft, quick healing.
No calluses, only the weakest shade of pink
across my knuckles,
wounds of deep thinking and rash movement.
When sleep comes, it's always a surprise.
My clothes still on the next morning,
sunrise
telling me it's time to see y'all again.

PORCHING IT UP
for Caleb

It's cold enough to blow smoke rings without the cigars,
but I'm not above suffering a little.
Remember the time we invented wisdom,
cracked our heads open and looked up,
gathered all the problems of the world
into one utterable sum? I don't, either,
but I feel like we can try.
A freezing gust of epiphone,
sage directions for the hunt,
the golden words of impossibly old men
hovering in our vaulted skulls
like steam, escaping however it can.

BETWEEN IZUMO AND YOUR BEDROOM

Your mind is playing tricks
on both of us. If my fingers
feel like maggots
it is because they come to life
on fresh meat
and tend to fester at night
in the dampest places.
Put your comb away,
all sacrifices burned
in the candles and rose quartz
melodies, stop whistling.
It's too late for all that
fire and whatever else
your head is swimming toward.
I have eaten all your food
and left you with a dusty stove
to boil fat, but with no more bones
to throw in.
I'll be back.
Hairs on your pillow,
air around your reflection and every bed
you find. Wake up to shake the thought
and I will still be the cold
in your toes
and the burner
you're sure, but not so sure
you turned off before you went to sleep.

WILL YOU SIGN MY YEARBOOK

for Jennifer

Long sleeves, dusk-eyed effervescence,
the kind of charm that whispers as it strikes.
I remember you in corners,
taking shade in the quiet
as you let big ideas
crash and recede around you,
playing fast and loose
with your silent attention.

I said your name
just to hear the truth confirmed.
Here you are
and that means I'm here, too,
that if you can acknowledge my existence,
maybe it's a good thing I exist.

GENESIS

Old dudes talk about posterity,
a four-dollar word for who's gonna come along
and fuck all this up. Ecclesiastical grunts
supported by few facts and a lot of wind.

Weird how we romanticize the past,
yet hang the future to dry
from our most predictable lengths of rope.

If success is measured in mimicry,
count me out, walk me to the gibbet,
hear me whistle
as the floor beneath me vanishes.

STUCK IN THE MIDDLE

Detours sprout in a hurry.
I suddenly can't find my way out of town.
There's a long day ahead: missed turns,
corn nuts, stories
etched in the fence posts along the way,
helping me remember where to turn.

39 is closed, 54 is closed, 169, closed.
I take a county road and hope
it cuts through to the other side,
gets me out of this shoulderless stretch
of gravel and bleeding tires.
Corn to the left of me, soy to the right,
here I am, stuck dead center,
the middle of nowhere.

CACTI

What stern words for the sun,
a real tight point of view.
No one likes to be forgotten,
but then again,
blistered skin is a special calling,
and no one can blame a sentinel
for doing its job,
bringing fruit, color to the sand,
forever rejecting comfort,
cool drinks, days that don't require
cloud cover to relax you.

RIVERTOWNE

Picked my brother up from jail,
drove his ass south so he could cry in a Wal-mart,
slick-eyed wonder at the people,
the clothes hanging in every direction,
enough space to reach out his arms
and say "I know what I want for dinner."
He doesn't sleep, he paces across the hotel room,
chugging complimentary coffee
and mumbling future plans,
making them up as he goes.

Tomorrow, his life starts fresh.
As long as I'm willing to drive him
as far from home as possible.
They can heal anyone down in Arkansas,
dip their heels in Lake Dardanelle,
immortality restored.
It worked for me, too.
On the way back,
one small stop off I-40,
God's purest work:
spare ribs
and the best potato salad I've ever eaten.

GARDENING TOOLS

Spare time is such a brightly buttered lie,
sustenance made to leave you starving,
you got nothing done, though you promised
you'd learn to nap the day away,
measure your weekend in boxed wine
and buffalo wings, delivery tips,
base instincts, relaxed muscles,
and thoughts reckoned from pure delight.

But it never seems to move.
You dig up fifteen fresh minutes
and it crumbles in your hand
all dried out, shovel-scarred,
tired from a long week spent spreading roots.
Fuck sleep and her sisters, all modes
of thought that lean against restful heads
and balanced breath. Don't look
for friends that won't come looking for you.
Bloodshot, but eager,
your eyes will see light wherever they need to.

SUMMER

Eddy set up a bucket
and filled it with water.
He chucked in one lit firecracker
at a time, ooh-ed and ah-ed
at this new found power
to get something moving
with his own hands.

The rest of us were too busy
for such selfish distractions.
We were caught up in the dreamy heat,
the swimming pool,
melon slices and lemonade,
beer cans that float right beside you,
make you forget
any worn out longing
for control.

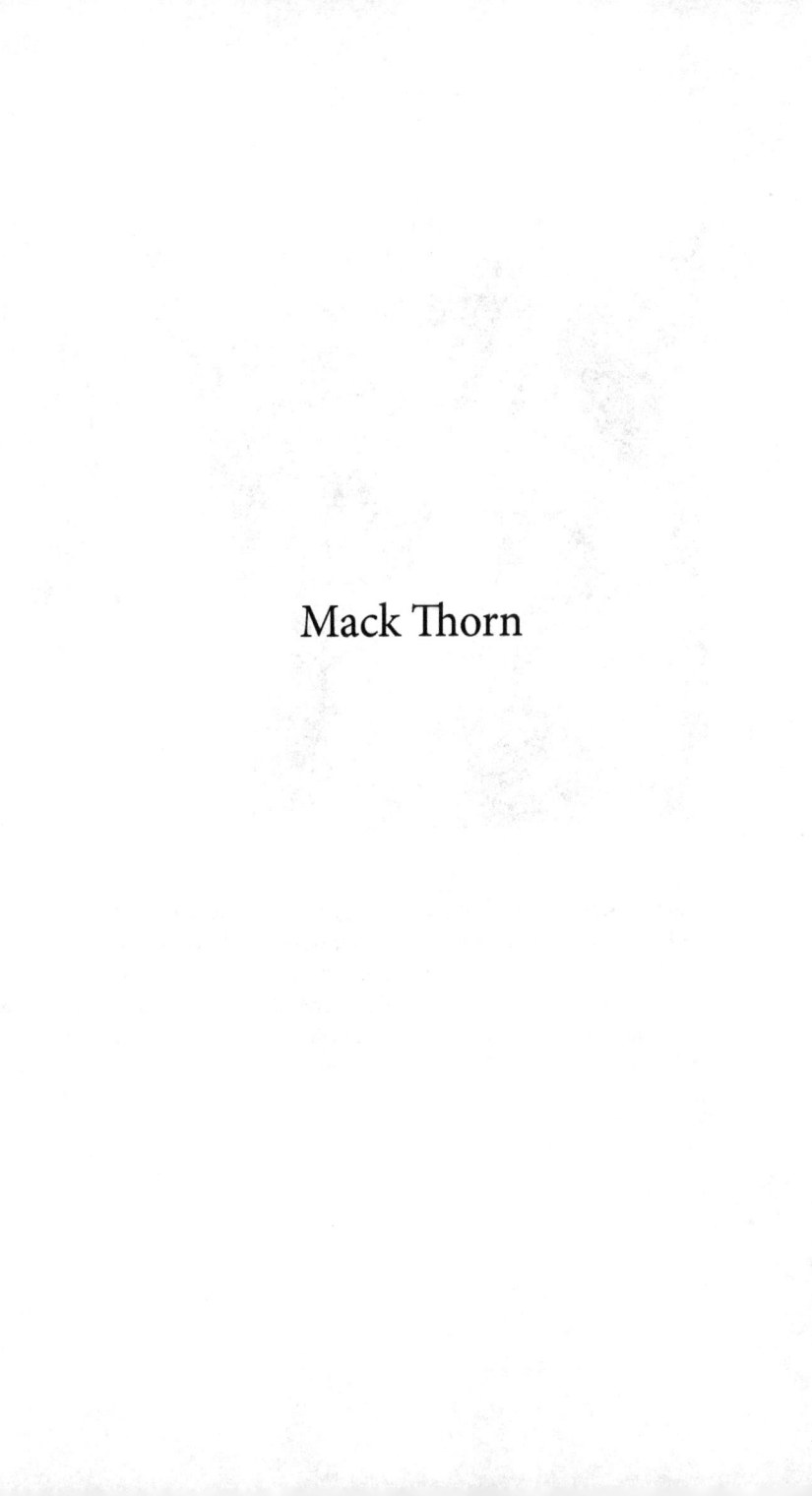

Mack Thorn

Mack Thorn is poet from St. Louis, Missouri. Growing up he has lived in almost every corner, nook, and cranny of his home town. Worked a broad array of conventional and unconventional jobs like drug rehabilitation and dry wall hanging. He also spent 6 years in the navy reserve. Published works in *Badjacket* zine and the *Whiskey Rye Review*.

One Armed Forklift Driver

If you're from around here
you may find it hard
to spell
by sounding out the words

or run
from the green vines
that entangle
the red brick
like a mighty python

around here
giving up
is the best thing
you could ever
do for yourself

a town filled
with amputated dreams
an arm given
for every classroom daydream
strong enough to grow wings
and fly high above
the steel mill smokestacks

go look in the warehouses in pontoon
and you'll see
all the one-armed forklift drivers
driving in circles
because they've forgotten how to turn around.

Whatever You Do Don't Get Old

To me
you will never
grow old

my sweet seraphim
with your smile
that shines
and eyes that sing
holy
holy
holy

locked away safe
in the part of my brain
where my memories sleep.

A Noble Last Stand

It's January
and I come home
from the pool hall
after sharing a few beers
with a spider web hand tattoo

as I begin to jingle keys
under a single streetlight
I hear behind me
not far away
nor close enough to see
a pack of coyotes
cackling and hollering
like a rebel yell
before a bayonet charge

and the growling cries of a dog
surrounded an outnumbered
defending his homestead
from the hungry winter invaders

from what I could hear
the dog fought valiantly
and with honor in his final moments
like the unnamed Viking
at the battle of Stamford bridge

although the night is dark
and the ground is cold
one day
I hope to meet you
in Valhalla
to shake your paw
my furry champion.

What Makes a Good Bar?

A good bar
like a good church
will be open
on Christmas eve
during a snowstorm
or most major holidays
when its parishioners
need shelter
and communion

but
a bad church
will turn off its lights
and close its doors
in the middle of
a hurricane.

Lift Kit Rain Dance

Across the street
from my bungalow
a pack of wild
revving diesel engines
howl
at the stars
and crescent moon
like a lift kit rain dance
before they patrol
the gravel lots
sonic drive-ins
and back roads
to look for
some kind of break
from the droning white noise
of predictable breeding futures.

Ruby Ridge

On an early
September morning
I decided to walk
instead of drive
to the corner store
I needed supplies
for a full day of chicken fried rice
and sixteen-ounce cans

the sun slow cooked the sidewalk
until it was tender enough
for bare feet to chew on

I didn't notice the sirens
until they were all around me
coming from all sides and alleyways

the whole street was taped off
at the intersection of Gustine and Wyoming
an army of fatigues foaming at the mouth
surrounded a house half a block down

a woman still in her bathrobe
and curler tiara told me that
a man with a gun
was holding two people hostage
in his home

I turned back to the road
and kept it pushing
I didn't want to see what came next

had to walk an few extra blocks
to get around the tape and tanks
but I got what I needed
locked and loaded
with paper bag in hand
to hold out
in my own
ruby ridge.

Sky Levee

Pray for the sun
and for the fox
when they spoke out of turn
they were never asked at all

the bugle horn calls for blood and
stomping hooves drum the earth
summoning all the forest
to march in unison

here in the jungle
there is no shelter to be found
only unremitting moments
of sheer terror

murder is painted
upon the stock car in hobo code
the sky levee breaks
and the plains become
flooded with light.

Peoples Changes

On the road
we all know
right in front of the store
where we would get snacks
and ask some stranger
to buy us tall boys and blunt wraps

godfather tried to speak wisdom into the tadpoles
as their tails pistol whipped through the swamp land
puffed smoke from curbs
that sliced the air into dancing ribbons

story goes
he sat in one spot to long
and they caught him daydreaming
of a future for his children
a slug to the face
was enough to end the season

now black lane is filled with buckshot
and stockings filled with shotgun shells
I'll put money on your books
just in case I go

a GED will only get you so far kid
you might as well learn to weld.

Roommates

Yellow and black spider with legs spread across the web
sitting on the glass door that I use to go outside
and smoke my cigarettes
I think it's an orb weaver
I named her Maggie

she watches the door for bugs and meth heads
maybe I'll give her a gnat or two
as an offering for her service

I see her every day without question
and now that we've become familiar strangers
there is no point in exercising the formalities of
    morning greetings
a simple head nod will do just fine

one day
I come to my desk
and as I sit down
I noticed that Maggie was gone
a hungry bat must have taken her in the night

her home is still there though
glinting against the glass
in the early morning sunlight
and shaking in the wind

I could be wrong about her demise
maybe she found another lonely guy
to look after in the night

When My Well Went Dry

I don't like who you have become
love has made your mind weak
and dull from slashing at rocks
paranoid that the salt within them will dry your well

the well is indifferent to you
yet your religion is unwavering
and your prayer forthcoming

I know you feel lost
without the water from this well
although it is true
that without it
we will die from thirst but
it is not the only source from which to drink.

maybe someday,
you'll come back to the river
and admire its beauty and indifference
feeling satisfied.

Shake and Bake

Snowblind riding the asphalt dragon towards oblivion
following the yellow stripes along its scaled back
as I take fellowship with a mute spirit

I ramble on
ramble on
in these blackout days
and shake and bake nights
only looking back to check and see
if jeepers creepers is in my rearview

I haven't seen gray since the drunk tank
and the gravel in this holler doesn't count
it moves and changes shape but
the gray inside don't move for no one
not even the Ozark Samson

ride on till the county line
just another twenty miles and
another hundred and sixty till I reach Arkansas
I might not be there for the kid's first day of school
but I'll have pocket change for books and air force ones

chase after the sun
until it chases after you in the morning
days and nights don't mean much
while moving packs of glass
for doctors and saints

never weighed down by the past
not with these scale stops and cops
these days
It's easy to let go
If you only look at horizons.

Animal

Like a wounded animal backed into a corner
you must fight
your mouth tastes like copper
and your wounds reek of death
but now
you must fight
not for victory
but in spite
for spirit
God is calling you home
fight now
and rest in the afterlife.

I Hate My Screen Door

Connection
the nectar we seek
to share with the sun

lost in this sea of dirt that
rolls and folds over Navajo hills

I look towards the apparent horizon
to witness the earth and sky embrace
like fleeting lovers
that refuse to let the world end

the dismantling of love
has cost us dearly and soon
the earth will release the sky
from its desperate grip and
we will fall with the sky in tandem

close your eyes
and accept that
it's already too late.

Hunger and Loneliness

I like hummus
on bread
and vegetables
and things

some more sweet
than salty
filled with flavors
like garlic or pepper spice

I like my friends
on couches
and beaches
and things
filling my belly with laughter
and satisfying my soul

I savor these moments
before it all becomes bittersweet.

Bus Stop Advice

Don't carry bags
and don't rest
while the devil is awake

twist curls and plastic wrap
on porch steps
just to pay for the kid's way

gas sits in the palm
because two grams in the bush
is worth one in the hand

I heard the children of Montezuma
are putting on leather patches
all because the angels
kept the hungry from eating

these days
If you don't have thunder in your palm
you must have the blade of Michael
ready at all times
prepared to be served
and given to the witness

with all of us trying to eat
in the middle of a food desert
all you can do
is hunt.

A Sunny Kansas Afternoon

Anxious leaves tremble
at the end of shaky branches
at any moment
dismembered from its provider
yet this flora veil
is what protects the tree from the sun

another id accessory
making up for lack of gumption
and shading the mind
from ultra-violet rays
of the superego.

Red Meat Causes Alzheimer's

Real men
forget who they are
their children's name
and where they went
on their honeymoon

real men
let themselves
slowly drift with the tide
into the open ocean of insanity

real men
let arthritis kill their bones and joints
until they hobble and shake
like feeble leaves on a fall branch
with their backs groaning
and begging for morphine drips

real men
drink alone
piss blood
let their teeth rot
kick puppies
use compact bows
and walk away slowly from explosions

real men
complain about sovereignty
but follows a religion
that refers to him as a sheep.

real men
inhale exhaust smoke
directly from rusted exhaust pipes
until their lungs
turn alveolus into buttered popcorn
and flatten out like a cat
under a sunny window on a spring afternoon

real men
don't cry
they clench their fists in a tight ball
as their coagulated arteries

shriek
contort
and spasm
until it all
goes quiet
like a real man.

Pistol Whip Neurons

I miss dopamine
ketamine kisses
and the floating sundresses that drape
over confessions of patricide

if you got something to say
just say it
then play it
over and over
until the tape burst
like the levees in the ninth ward

my generation
has only known tragedy
we were all born under a bad sign

billowing smoke tickles helicopter propellers
only to be dismissed by the
bright
gawky
word of God

Stop groveling

he says

I'm a mistake and so are you.

You Got it All Wrong Kid

You read Camus
to look for a reason
to finish your finance degree

fantasize yourself
as a reflection of the stranger
because you're bitter
about being better off at birth

all I see is a whiteboy
that killed a brown one
in cold blood
and didn't get away with it.

The Great American Pyramid Scheme

Hacking butts and burning trail heads
from Canaan to Colorado
with doc martin creek stompers
on a horse named buddy

I listen close to the psalms of eagles
as they beckon for springs return
and the righteous wrath of an honorable man

chambered shotguns shells give chase
as I run from social castes
on a four-wheeler down an eight-lane superhighway
towards the big lotto check in the sky

atom bombs and polio
just don't bother soccer moms no more
but you can sure as shit
find one in a hospital gown coughing up a lung
because of what she read on the internet

can't say who's the bigger sucker
because we all got scammed into believing
that there are rules in this game we all play.

Lost Track of Time

Lost track of time,
it's quite easy to do
when the world is lost to the wandering eye

scatter a day or two in the topsoil
watch it grow from weeks to months
then years

harvest memories from picture frames
adjourned by hovering dust
amidst the winking setting sun

I wonder where the time went
what life I didn't live
how time just passed me by

a taste of want
leaves the body hungry
in banquet halls
filled with empty hearts

a life not lived
saved for a rainy day
waiting for another turn
another chance
to do it differently.

This project was made possible, in part, by generous support from the Osage Arts Community.

Osage Arts Community provides temporary time, space and support for the creation of new artistic works in a retreat format, serving creative people of all kinds — visual artists, composers, poets, fiction and nonfiction writers. Located on a 152-acre farm in an isolated rural mountainside setting in Central Missouri and bordered by ¾ of a mile of the Gasconade River, OAC provides residencies to those working alone, as well as welcoming collaborative teams, offering living space and workspace in a country environment to emerging and mid-career artists. For more information, visit us at www.osageac.org

Osage Arts Community